my first bisaya book

for kids

A Children's Introduction to the
Language and Culture

This book belongs to:

_____

table of Contents

Family

inahan (ee-NA-han)
mother

amahan (ah-MA-han)
father

manong (mah-NONG)
older brother

manang (mah-NANG)
older sister

lola (LO-la)
grandmother

lolo (LO-lo)
grandfather

bata (bA-ta)
baby

higala (hee-GA-la)
friend

Meal time

kaon (KAH-on)
eat

kutsara (koot-SA-ra)
spoon

tinidor (tee-NEE-dor)
fork

tasa (TA-sah)
cup

inom (EE-nom)
drink

3

plato (PLA-to)
plate

yahong (YA-hong)
bowl

lamesa (la-ME-sa)
table

bangko (BANG-ko)
chair

4

Food and Drinks

manga (MANG-ga)
mango

kapayas (ka-PA-yas)
papaya

pinya (PIN-ya)
pineapple

saging (sa-GING)
banana

utan (OO-tan)
vegetables

kamatis (ka-MA-tis)
tomato

patatas (pa-TA-tas)
potato

talong (ta-LONG)
eggplant

kalabasa (ka-la-BA-sa)
squash

6

luy-a (LOOY-a)
ginger

sibuyas (see-BOO-yas)
onion

ahos (A-hos)
garlic

sili (SEE-lee)
chili pepper

gatas (ga-TAS)
milk

pan (PAN)
bread

itlog (IT-log)
egg

kan-on (kahn-ON)
rice

8

Bath time

hugas (HOO-gas)
wash

gripo (GREE-po)
faucet

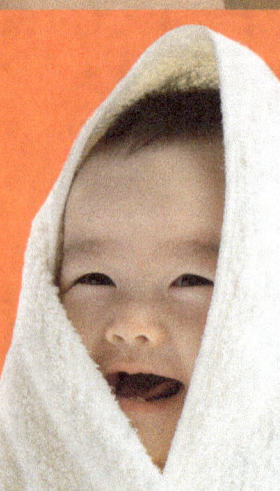

tualya (too-AL-ya)
towel

sabon (SA-bon)
soap

sudlay (SOOD-lai)
comb

balde (BAL-de)
pail

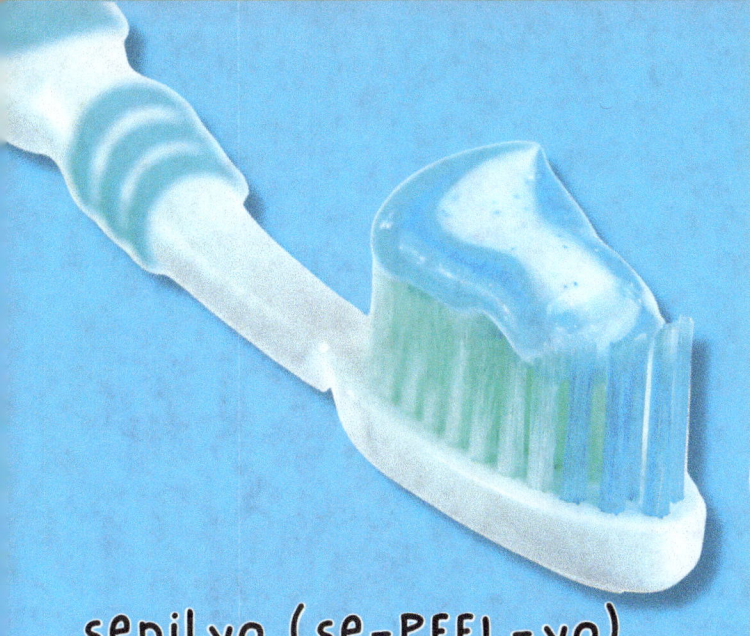

sepilyo (se-PEEL-yo)
toothbrush

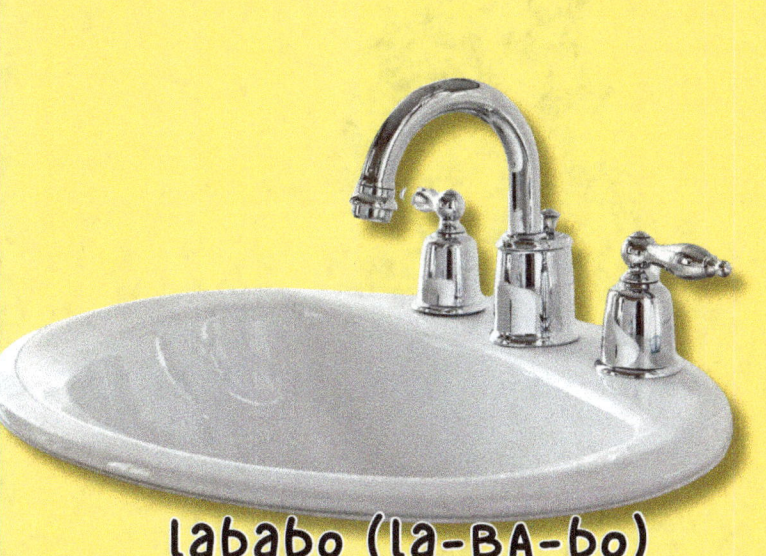

lababo (la-BA-bo)
sink

10

Sleep time

tulog (TOO-log)
sleep

katre (KAH-tre)
bed

unlan (OON-lan)
pillow

habol (HA-bol)
blanket

kutson (KUT-son)
mattress

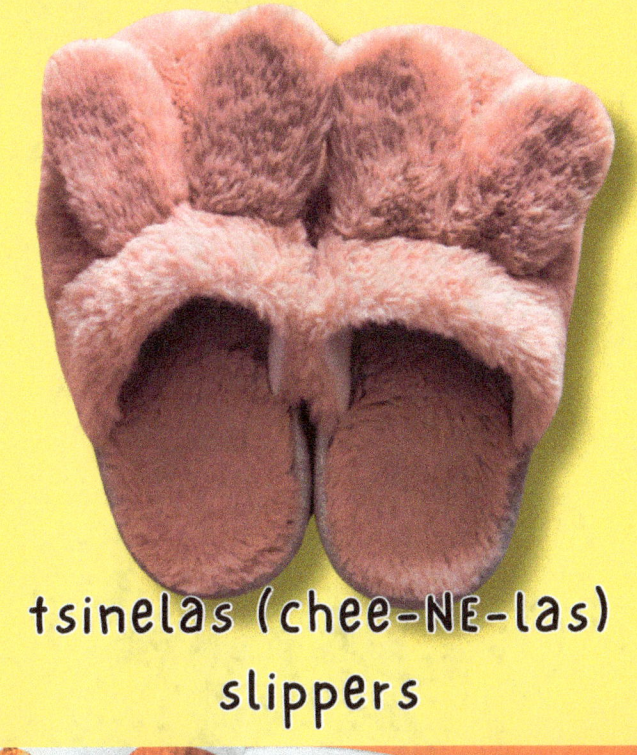

tsinelas (chee-NE-las)
slippers

kurtina (kur-TEE-na)
curtains

libro (LEE-bro)
book

12

Clothing

pantalon (pan-ta-LON)
pants

sayal (sah-YAHL)
skirt

medyas (MED-yas)
socks

sapatos (sa-PA-tos)
shoes

kurbata (kur-BA-ta)
tie

bakos (BAH-kos)
belt

guwantes (gwan-TES)
gloves

kapote (ka-PO-te)
raincoat

14

Numbers

usa (OO-sah)

one

duha (DOO-hah)

two

tulo (TOO-loh)

three

upat (oo-pat)

four

lima (LEE-mah)

five

15

unom (OO-nom)

six

pito (PEE-to)

seven

walo (WA-lo)

eight

siyam (SEE-yam)

nine

napulo (na-POO-lo)

ten

16

Colors

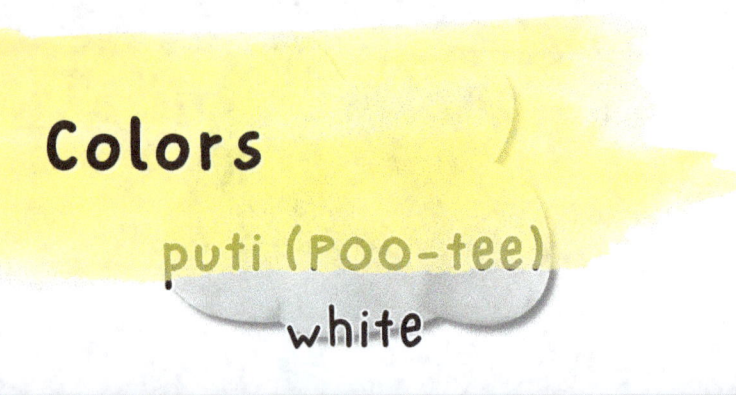

puti (POO-tee)
white

itom (EE-tom)
black

pula (POO-la)
red

kahel (KA-hel)
orange

dalag (DA-lag)
yellow

17

asul (AH-sul)
blue

berde (BER-de)
green

rosas (RO-sas)
pink

ube (oo-be)
purple

18

Nature and Environment

langit (LAH-ngit)
sky

bulan (boo-LAN)
moon

bitoon (bee-to-on)
star

adlaw (AD-law)
sun

kahoy (ka-HOY)
tree

bulak (boo-LAK)
flower

dahon (DA-hon)
leaf

bato (BA-to)
stone

20

Body Parts

ulo (OO-lo)
head

mata (MA-ta)
eye

ilong (EE-LONG)
nose

buhok (boo-HOK)
hair

dalunggan (da-LUNG-gan)
ear

ngipon (NGEE-pon)
teeth

dila (DEE-la)
tongue

tuhod (TOO-hod)
knee

kamot (KA-mot)
hand

tiil (TEE-il)
foot

22

Animals

iro (EE-roh)
dog

iring (EE-ring)
cat

isda (EES-da)
fish

langgam (LANG-gam)
bird

23

kabayo (ka-BA-yo)
horse

baboy (BA-boy)
pig

manok (ma-NOK)
chicken

baki (ba-KEE)
frog

24

kanding (KAN-ding)
goat

ilaga (ee-LA-ga)
ilaga

kuneho (koo-NE-ho)
rabbit

25

pato (PAH-to)
duck

buyog (BOO-yog)
bee

tiki (TEE-kee)
lizard

ulod (OO-lod)
worm

halas (HA-las)
snake

Everyday objects

orasan (o-RA-san)
clock

telepono (te-le-PO-no)
phone

bintana (bin-TA-na)
window

purtahan (pur-TA-han)
door

yabi (YA-bi)
key

samin (SAH-min)
mirror

**bentilador
(ben-tee-LAH-dor)**
electric fan

suga (SOO-ga)
light

28

transportation

sakyanan (sak-YA-nan)
car

bisikleta (bee-sik-LE-ta)
bicycle

motor (mo-TOR)
motorcycle

sikad (SEE-kad)
tricycle

29

bangka (BANG-ka)
boat

barko (BAR-ko)
ship

eroplano (er-RO-pla-no)
airplane

30

Action Words

dula (DOO-la)
play

dagan (DAH-gan)
run

lakaw (LAH-kaw)
walk

lingkod (LING-kod)
sit

tindog (tin-DOG)
stand

ambak (AM-bak)
jump

pakpak (PAK-pak)
clap

katawa (ka-TA-wa)
laugh

32

Emotions

lipay (LEE-pay)
happy

suko (SOO-ko)
angry

hadlok (HAD-lok)
scared

kurat (KOO-rat)
surprised

kapoy (KA-poy)
tired

gutom (GOO-tom)
hungry

uhaw (oo-haw)
thirsty

ulaw (oo-law)
shy

34

I'd love to hear from you...

Did your child enjoy exploring the Bisaya language with us? We'd love to hear about your child's experience with "My First Bisaya Book for Kids" Your feedback will help us support other families on their language learning journey.

https://go.binnovatedigital.com/BisayaBookbowker

Please scan the QR code with your phone camera, or copy the link on your phone or computer browser.

I am immensely grateful for your time. Daghang Salamat!

Love,

Emma